The Great Mississippi Flood of 1927

CORNERSTONES OF FREEDOM

SECOND SERIES

Deborah Kent

Children's Press®
A Division of Scholastic Inc.
New York • Toronto • London • Auckland • Sydney
Mexico City • New Delhi • Hong Kong
Danbury, Connecticut

Photographs © 2007: Corbis Images: 18 (Norman W. Alley/Bettmann), 20 (D. A. Arrivee), 3 (Bettmann), 12 left (Mathew B. Brady Studio/Medford Historical Society Collection), 6 (Royalty-Free), cover bottom right; Getty Images/Hulton Archive: 40 (MPI), 32; Herbert Hoover Presidential Library: 39, 45 right; HQ, USACE, Office of History: 14, 16; Library of Congress: 12 right (Williams & Cornwell), 4, 5, 10, 15, 19, 21, 25, 28, 29, 30, 35, 37, 44 bottom, 44 top right; National Archives and Records Administration: 11 (Great Lakes Region-Chicago), cover top left, 24, 26; National Geographic Image Collection: 22, 27, 31, 33, 45 left; North Wind Picture Archives: 9, 44 top left; The Image Works/Andre Jenny: 8, 41.

Map by XNR Productions, Inc.

Library of Congress Cataloging-in-Publication Data
Kent, Deborah.
  The great Mississippi flood of 1927 / Deborah Kent.
      p. cm. — (Cornerstones of Freedom. Second series)
  Includes bibliographical references and index.
  ISBN-10: 0-516-23628-8
  ISBN-13: 978-0-516-23628-5
 1. Floods—Mississippi River—History—20th century—Juvenile literature. 2. Mississippi River—History—20th century—Juvenile literature. 3. Floods—Mississippi River Valley—History—20th century—Juvenile literature. 4. Mississippi River Valley—History—1865—Juvenile literature. I. Title. II. Series.
  F354.K46 2006
  977'.03—dc22   2005007524

1 2 3 4 5 6 7 8 9 10 R 16 15 14 13 12 11 10 09 08 07

On the night of April 20, 1927, a crew of 450 men worked in a raging downpour near the town of Mound Landing, Mississippi, located 12 miles (19 kilometers) north of Greenville. Some of the men stuffed large sacks with dirt and sand. Others hauled the heavy sandbags to the top of the **levee**, a massive earthen wall that ran along the Mississippi River.

Rising water can create crevasses—breaks in a levee that allow river waters to flood the land.

After months of heavy rain, the river had reached the top of the levee, which rose some 30 feet (9 meters) above the ground. By adding layers of sandbags, the workers tried to heighten the levee and prevent a disastrous flood.

The rising river put tremendous pressure on the levee, and any weak point could lead to a break, known as a **crevasse**. Early on the morning of April 21, water began streaming through a small tear at the top of the levee. As workers frantically piled on more sandbags, the stream became a torrent. It swept away the sandbags as if they were chips of wood. As the men watched, the hole yawned wider and deeper. The great levee shivered beneath their feet.

"You could see the earth just start boiling," recalled Moses Mason, one of the workers. "A man hollered, 'Watch out! It's gonna break!' Everybody was hollering to get off. It was like turning a hydrant on—water was shooting forward."

★ ★ ★ ★

Whenever parts of the
levee collapsed, great
damage followed. The
flooding water destroyed
everything in its path.

With a mighty roar, the river burst through the levee, its deadly power unleashed at last. The flood carried away everything in its path—trees, barns, houses, animals, and terrified human beings.

For more than four months—since January 1927—crews had been working desperately to strengthen all the levees up and down the Mississippi and its **tributaries**, or branches. Time after time, the force of the river defeated human efforts. Wherever portions of the levee collapsed, the river flooded thousands of acres of land and drowned countless men, women, and children. In loss of life and

This photograph shows a portion of the Mississippi and its tributaries, which extend like the branches of a tree.

property, the great Mississippi River flood of 1927 was one of the worst natural disasters in the history of the United States.

"THE FATHER OF WATERS"

On a map, the Mississippi River resembles a tree. The "trunk" of the tree stretches north from the river's mouth at the Gulf of Mexico to its source in Minnesota's Lake Itasca. The tree's many "branches" are the river's tributaries, which spread across much of the North American continent. Tributaries in the Mississippi River system include the Ohio, the Tennessee, the Arkansas, the

Missouri, the Red, the Illinois, the North Platte, the South Platte, and the Yellowstone. With its sprawling tributaries, the Mississippi touches thirty-one of the fifty states. Only two other river systems on Earth—Africa's Congo and the Amazon of South America—are larger. It is little wonder that the native people of North America called the Mississippi "the Father of Waters."

From the Rocky Mountains in the west, from the Appalachian mountain chain in the east, and from the prairies in the Midwest, water flows ceaselessly into the main trunk of the Mississippi. Tons of earth, pebbles, and sand are washed toward the Gulf of Mexico by this never-ending flow.

The mouth of the Mississippi River is located at the Gulf of Mexico. The river stretches north to its source in Minnesota's Lake Itasca.

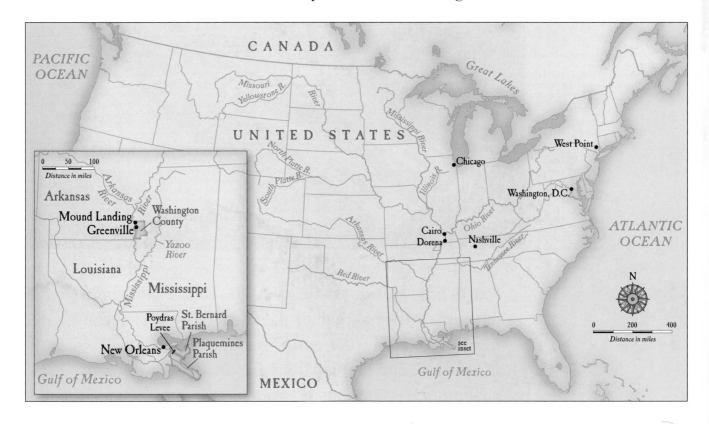

A view of the Mississippi River in St. Louis, Missouri, showing its dark-brown color.

This debris, known as **silt**, gives the river a dark-brown color and earns it the nickname "the Big Muddy." Geologists—scientists who study the earth—estimate that the Mississippi deposits several million tons of silt along its lower course each day. Over millions of years, these silt deposits formed a flat, fertile **delta** stretching for hundreds of miles.

8

TAMING THE RIVER

From 1539 to 1543, Spanish explorer Hernando de Soto led an expedition across the region that is now the southeastern United States. On May 8, 1541, de Soto and his men were the first Europeans to see the Mississippi River in its **channel**. In his journal, one of the men in de Soto's party described a Mississippi flood: "[The great river] came down with an enormous increase of water. . . . Soon it began to flow over the fields in an immense flood, and as the land was level, without any hills, there was nothing to stop [it]."

By the early 1700s, Europeans began to build permanent settlements along the Mississippi's banks. The delta provided the richest farmland the settlers had ever seen. Wealthy planters raised sugar and rice. During the 1800s, cotton became their chief crop. Many planters, particularly

SNAGS ON THE RIVER

In addition to silt, the Mississippi carries tree branches and even huge logs. Tangled clumps of branches and logs are known as **snags**. In the early nineteenth century, a huge snag in the Red River, one of the Mississippi's tributaries, extended nearly 40 miles (64 km).

Hernando de Soto and his men were the first Europeans to explore the Mississippi River. Years later many Europeans would settle along the Mississippi's banks.

This photo from 1910 shows a levee that has been constructed to protect New Orleans from flooding. For years, people believed levees alone would protect the city.

the French, depended on black slaves to sow, tend, and harvest their crops.

Most of the time, the river flowed quietly beside towns and plantations, a sleepy giant content to live at peace with its human neighbors. Every few years, however, spring brought unusually heavy rainfall. Then the giant awoke and set loose another devastating flood upon the land.

New Orleans was founded near the mouth of the Mississippi, in present-day Louisiana, in 1718. After a series of floods, the people of New Orleans attempted to tame the river. In 1726, they built levees to protect their town when the river rose. The first levees were built of earth and stood 4 to 6 feet (1 to 2 m) high. As settlement expanded, more and more miles of levees were constructed.

People who study the river and develop flood-prevention methods are called engineers. Some early engineers believed that levees alone could control the river. Others believed that additional methods of flood control should be used. They thought that reservoirs could hold an overflow of water. Trenches called **spillways** could be connected to the river. When a flood threatened, the spillways could carry off some of the excess water and reduce pressure on the levees. The debate on whether or not to build more flood controls raged for nearly two centuries.

Control of the river became a lifelong passion for two nineteenth-century engineers, Andrew Atkinson Humphreys and James Buchanan Eads. Eads believed that higher levees would force the river to flow faster. He thought that a faster current would scour the riverbed, washing away much of the silt and allowing large ships to pass.

The Ogee Spillway is an example of a spillway, a method of carrying off excess water to reduce pressure on levees.

Andrew Atkinson Humphreys (above) and James Buchanan Eads (right), two nineteenth-century engineers, believed that levees alone could not prevent flooding of the Mississippi.

Humphreys became chief of the Army Corps of Engineers after the Civil War (1861–1865). The corps was in charge of building many of the levees along the Mississippi. Humphreys spent eleven years writing a massive scientific report about the river. In his report, known as the Delta Survey, he described in detail the complex currents that flowed through every section of the lower Mississippi (from Cairo,

Illinois, to the Gulf of Mexico). Engineers used the Delta Survey well into the twentieth century.

Humphreys and Eads were bitter rivals who agreed on very little. They did agree on one thing: Levees alone could not prevent flooding on the Mississippi. Both believed that spillways and other outlets should serve as a backup.

In 1879, the U.S. Congress created the Mississippi River Commission, a body of civil and military engineers, to control the river. However, the commission paid little attention to scientific evidence. Instead, it concerned itself with cutting costs and pleasing politicians. Its members ignored the advice of Humphreys, Eads, and others who had firsthand experience with the river.

To prevent flooding, the Mississippi River Commission chose to depend on levees alone. Although they drew different conclusions, commission members followed Eads's thinking. They argued that a strong system of levees would hold the river tightly within its banks and force it to flow more swiftly. The increased current would scour away much of the accumulated silt and thus deepen the riverbed. Ships would be able to travel more easily up and down the waters. The federal government was willing to pay for levee construction on the grounds that it would encourage shipping on the Mississippi.

TOUCHING BOTTOM

When James Buchanan Eads was twenty-two years old, he invented a **diving bell** that enabled human beings to explore the bottom of the river. A supply of air was trapped within the bell as it descended, permitting the diver to breathe. Eads described his first trip to the bottom of the Mississippi: "The sand was drifting like a dense snowstorm. . . . I could feel . . . the sand rushing past my hands, driven by a current apparently as rapid as that on the surface. I could discover the sand in motion at least two feet [1 m] below the surface of the bottom."

When the levees broke, the flowing water was so powerful that homes and buildings were destroyed.

For the next fifty years, the Mississippi River Commission oversaw the building and maintenance of levees along the Mississippi and its branches. It also closed off a number of creeks and other natural outlets that normally funneled some water out of the river. Despite these measures, silt deposits continued to build. These deposits raised the bottom of the river higher each year. As the river grew shallower, work crews built the levees steadily higher to hold it in check.

THE RESTLESS WATERS

Though the levees rose taller and taller, disastrous floods still occurred along the Mississippi. In 1882, 1903, 1913, and again in 1922, levees crumbled and water poured across thousands of acres of farmland. A number of engineers challenged the levees-only policy of the Mississippi River Commission. They called for studies on the use of spillways and reservoirs. One report acknowledged that a system of spillways might help prevent floods, but concluded that such a system would be too

The strength of the floodwaters caused the levees to slide, resulting in deep fissures in the earth.

★ ★ ★ ★

costly. The commissioners insisted that spillways would seldom be needed as long as the levees stayed strong.

After the 1922 flood, the battered levees were mended and built higher than ever before. During the summer of 1926, General Edgar Jadwin, chief of the Army Corps of Engineers, gave his annual report. Jadwin declared that, for the first time, the levees were fully equipped "to prevent the destructive effects of floods."

The sight of the levees was impressive indeed. A massive earthen wall guarded each side of the lower Mississippi River, stretching 1,100 miles (1,770 km) from Cairo, Illinois, to the Gulf of Mexico. The levees began 1 mile (2 km) back from the river's natural banks, leaving a broad floodplain called the **batture**. The batture was planted with willows and other trees to keep the riverbank from eroding. Between the batture and the levee ran the **barrow pit**, a

In 1926, General Edgar Jadwin, chief of the Army Corps of Engineers, declared that the levees were equipped to handle the destructive effects of floods.

16

trench about 300 feet (91 m) wide and 14 feet (4 m) deep. The barrow pit helped to accommodate water when the river overflowed. Earth was taken from the barrow pit to build up the levee.

The levee itself was an immense, sloping ridge of earth 30 feet (9 m) high. Built to strict standards, it measured 188 feet (57 m) thick at the base and 8 feet (2 m) across at the crown, or top. The entire levee was planted with a tough ground cover called Bermuda grass. The dense roots of the Bermuda grass helped to hold the earth in place. It was almost inconceivable that the river could threaten such an immense structure. Yet the river in flood stage—the giant awakened—had ferocious power. It could menace the strongest levees built by human hands.

RIVER RISING

In August 1926, just weeks after General Jadwin promised that the levees were secure, heavy storms swirled over the Midwest. The summer had been long and hot. At first, people welcomed the rain. But as the days turned into weeks, one storm followed another. From Nebraska and South Dakota to Kentucky and Ohio, farmers' fields flooded and crops were destroyed. The upper Mississippi, from Minnesota to southern Illinois, rose steadily. The rain continued to fall through September and October.

When the storms finally ceased in the Midwest, savage blizzards swept in to take their place. Meanwhile, heavy rains began to deluge the South. The Cumberland River overflowed and flooded Nashville, Tennessee. In the state

A photographer takes a break from capturing the raging Illinois River in 1922. This flood, like the one in 1927, washed out railroad tracks and flooded farmland.

of Mississippi, a flood on the Yazoo River left hundreds of people homeless. Swollen and angry, the Mississippi rolled southward, fenced between its towering levees. The weight of billions of tons of water thrust against the earthen walls, trying to break through to the other side, was unimaginable.

Early in February 1927, levees gave way on the White and Little Red rivers in Arkansas. As much as 10 feet (3 m) of water buried 100,000 acres (40,468 hectares) of land. All along the lower Mississippi, people worried that other levees would fail. The chairman of the Mississippi River Commission tried to reassure the public. He said that, although the river stood at record levels for that time of year, "no serious trouble with floodwaters is expected this spring unless

MEASURING THE FLOOD

Flood conditions on a river are measured in cubic feet per second (cfs), which means the number of cubic feet of water flowing each second at a particular spot. A cubic foot is a square 1 foot (.3 m) long, 1 foot (.3 m) wide, and 1 foot (.3 m) high. In 1927, engineers estimated that the levees on the Mississippi could handle 1.5 million cfs. As the water rose, however, it reached 3 million cfs in many places.

Men worked to save the levee outside Lakeport, Arkansas, by laying wooden planks on the slope and then covering them with sandbags. This fight succeeded, but only because a levee on the other side broke.

This logger in Idaho is digging a hole around a tree so he can cut it down. Heavy winter snowfall like this, which melted in spring, increased the river's level.

more rain than usual falls." The storms did not subside. From Tennessee to the Gulf of Mexico, the skies let loose still more rain throughout March. Further west, fresh blizzards dumped heavy snow from Montana to Texas.

Already the levees were enduring incredible strain. As the winter snows melted and spring rains began, the river rose still higher. Local organizers prepared to heighten and strengthen the levees. They ordered trainloads of empty cotton sacks, which could be used to make sandbags. They bought power generators and thousands of strings of lights to shine on the levees at night. Work would go on twenty-four hours a day.

This photo shows a levee in East Newport, Arkansas. As the water rises on both sides, the levee is narrowing.

Thousands of laborers were needed to build up the levees and reinforce them against breaks. Ever since the era of slavery, many white planters in the South had depended heavily on the labor of blacks. In the 1920s, millions of blacks worked as **sharecroppers** on large farms or plantations. When laborers were needed on the levees, plantation owners sent their sharecroppers to help complete the exhausting and dangerous work.

When laborers were needed to build up the levees, thousands of black sharecroppers did the long, dangerous work of trying to keep the river under control.

By April, some 30,000 black men were working on the levees. Work crews consisted of 100 to 200 laborers, directed by a single white foreman. At most work sites, the foremen were armed with pistols. Rumors spread up and down the levees about foremen who shot "troublemakers" and shoved their bodies into the river.

While the workers struggled to pile on sandbags, guards patrolled the levees around the clock. There was always the possibility that someone would purposely try to damage one of the levees. If the levee gave way on one side of the river, the pressure would ease and the levee on the opposite bank would be safe. To protect his or her property, someone from one side might decide to dynamite the levee on the other side. The guards were ordered to shoot to kill if they saw any person approach the levee without permission.

WORKING THE LAND

Under the system known as sharecropping, people who didn't own land rented land from wealthy planters. They served as laborers, planting and tending the landowner's crops. The landowner loaned the sharecropper money to pay his expenses during the year. The sharecropper was allowed to plant his own crops on a piece of the landowner's property. When the sharecropper sold his crops, he was expected to pay back the money to the landowner. Usually the sharecropper was so deeply in debt that he had no money left after paying off his loans. Thus, sharecroppers became trapped in an endless cycle of debt and poverty.

DISASTER ON THE DELTA

On April 16, the Mississippi ripped out nearly 1/2 mile (.8 km) of levee near Dorena, Missouri. Soon more levees collapsed—in Illinois, Missouri, Arkansas, and Tennessee. Red Cross volunteers worked frantically to feed and shelter thousands of **refugees**, people left homeless by the disaster. The storms raged on, and the river kept rising.

In Washington County, Mississippi, laborers worked feverishly to reinforce the levee. One of the weakest spots

A family stands in the windows of their home, which was flooded by the Mississippi River.

On April 21, the levee at Mound Landing broke. One plantation owner witnessed a wall of water 7 feet (2 m) high approach his home outside of Greenville, Mississippi.

was at Mound Landing, where a bend in the river sent water crashing against the levee with astounding force. On April 20, a Washington County businessman wrote in his diary, "Stormy tonight with gales blowing and rain threatened every moment. Hard on levees. Heaven spare us." Lashed by the wind, the water beat constantly at the levee. At last, the next day, the levee at Mound Landing could bear the strain no longer. A 100-foot (30-m)-long portion of the levee was pushed out when the levee finally broke. Steadily, the water slowly moved south, at a rate of 14 miles (22 km) a day. Bells tolled and fire whistles wailed a dire warning. Mules brayed, cows bellowed, and dogs howled. Families

THE CREST OF THE FLOOD

As a river rises, the water forms one or more swiftly moving waves, or **crests**. The crest is the point where the moving water is at its highest. After heavy rains, crests may form in a number of places at once. Observers carefully note the height of each crest and how fast it is traveling.

A man, standing on floating wreckage, and a dog (foreground) await rescue while surrounded by floodwater.

grabbed the few possessions they could carry and fled the advancing water. Some people perched in treetops or clung to the roofs of houses. Thousands streamed toward the remaining portion of the levee. It was the only land within miles that stood above the flood. A black woman named Cora Walker remembered, "Just as we got to the levee we turned back and saw our house turned over. We could see our own place tumbling, hear our things falling down. . . . Every time the waves came the levee would shake like you were in a rocking chair."

The flood turned thousands of ordinary people into heroes. In fishing boats, rowboats, and yachts searchers braved the swirling sea that had once been lush delta farm-land. They rescued shivering flood victims from roofs,

★ ★ ★ ★

Families built makeshift rafts and took with them only possessions they could carry.

trees, and rafts of floating wreckage. Fourteen-year-old John Tigrett ran rescue missions in an outboard motorboat. "Every day we had assigned certain routes," he recalled later. "We'd go out, pick these people up, bring them to the high ground and keep going." Blacks rescued whites and whites rescued blacks, setting aside racial barriers.

The Mound Landing crevasse flooded an area of the Mississippi Delta 60 miles (97 km) wide and 100 miles (161 km) long. No one knows how many people drowned, their bodies swept away forever. More than 180,000 people, most of them black and poor, lost their homes. The Red Cross cared for tens of thousands in makeshift shelters, including warehouses, stores, and railroad boxcars. Some 13,000 people took shelter on the levee near the town of Greenville, Mississippi. The levee—all of 8 feet (2.5 m) wide and 8 miles (13 km) long—became its own city, teeming with people.

RED CROSS TO THE RESCUE

Clara Barton, a nurse who had cared for wounded soldiers during the Civil War, founded the American Red Cross in 1881. The Red Cross offers help to people whose lives are disrupted by war or natural disasters. After storms, fires, floods, or earthquakes, Red Cross volunteers rush to the scene. They provide food, clothing, and shelter, helping survivors to rebuild their lives.

27

The Red Cross set up makeshift shelters where thousands of victims could seek some relief.

As the floodwaters rolled away from the crevasse, they gradually spread and lowered. Eventually, the water encountered higher ground and could go no further. Instead, it began to pour back toward the riverbed. Much of the water that caused such damage in Washington County later returned to the Mississippi—and headed south toward New Orleans.

With nearly half a million people, New Orleans was the cultural and financial center of the lower Mississippi. The city had battled floods for more than two centuries. Now the people of New Orleans lived in dread of the most catastrophic flood in history.

Engineers and weather experts were confident that the levees around New Orleans would protect the city. Crevasses further north had lessened the force of the river, so the high water could flow harmlessly out to sea. But the people of New Orleans were not convinced. Too many reassuring predictions had already proved false.

A group of powerful New Orleans bankers worried that a flood, or even the threat of a flood, would ruin business in the city. Investors might withdraw their money from New Orleans banks and companies. The city's business leaders decided to take action. To ease pressure on the levees at New Orleans, they decided to dynamite the Poydras

New Orleans was the cultural and financial center of the lower Mississippi. Business leaders scrambled to save it from the devastating flood.

Levee at Caernarvon, 13 miles (21 km) further south. Thousands of acres of marshland would be flooded in mostly rural St. Bernard and Plaquemines **parishes**. (In Louisiana, a county is called a parish.) The marshes could absorb the floodwaters, and New Orleans would be spared.

The people of St. Bernard and Plaquemines parishes were poor and uneducated. Many were black. Others were "Islenos," the descendants of immigrants from the Canary Islands off the coast of Spain. Trapping mink and muskrats for their pelts was the main industry in the marshes. If the land was flooded, these people would lose their homes and their livelihood.

Leaders from the endangered parishes pleaded with city officials, state lawmakers, and even the governor of Louisiana. Despite their efforts, plans to dynamite the levee moved ahead. Business leaders promised that the people of St. Bernard and Plaquemines would be **compensated**, or repaid, for the losses they suffered. Some 10,000 people were evacuated. They went to stay with friends or relatives, or moved into a New Orleans warehouse that served as a shelter.

People along the Mississippi River delta, including this man holding muskrat pelts, made their living along the river. When the river flooded, people's challenge was no longer making a living, but surviving.

On April 29, as reporters and spectators watched in excitement, the first explosion blasted a hole in the levee. A sluggish stream of water began to flow through the break. It took 39 tons of dynamite, used over a period of ten days, to create a full-scale flood over the marshes. St. Bernard sheriff L. A. Meraux told a group of reporters, "Gentlemen, you have seen today the public execution of this parish."

30

Men used posthole diggers to plant dynamite to blow up a levee to save the town of New Orleans.

THE POLITICS OF KINDNESS

By the end of April 1927, floodwaters sprawled over 26,000 square miles (67,340 square km) of land, an area the size of Connecticut, Massachusetts, New Hampshire, and Vermont combined. Nearly half a million people were left homeless.

★ ★ ★ ★

The American people were deeply moved by the plight of the flood victims. Storekeepers and factory owners donated money toward relief efforts. Schoolchildren collected clothing and canned goods. Thousands of people joined the Red Cross as volunteers. They brought food, blankets, and other supplies to homeless families from Missouri to Louisiana.

President Calvin Coolidge appointed Secretary of Commerce Herbert Hoover to coordinate rescue and relief programs. Hoover would oversee the work of the Red Cross and a host of local relief organizations. He could even issue orders to the U.S. Army and U.S. Navy.

Herbert Hoover seemed the perfect man for the job. He had coordinated relief efforts for European refugees during and after World War I (1914–1918). His skill at planning and his ability to bring people together had saved countless lives. The great Mississippi flood presented him with a new set of challenges.

Traveling by train and boat, Hoover inspected flood damage and refugee camps up and down the river. He met with rescue teams and Red Cross coordinators. He worked to organize a food distribution network to deliver supplies as swiftly as possible. Wherever he went, Hoover was followed by a band of reporters. His work on behalf of the flood survivors made headlines across the land.

Of all the places hit by the flood, none suffered greater loss of life and property than Washington County, Mississippi. William Alexander Percy, son of a prominent banker and cotton grower, directed the countywide relief efforts. Percy decided that the thirteen thousand black refugees stranded on the levee must be evacuated. He arranged for steamboats to take them to dry land.

Will Percy's father, LeRoy Percy, was the most powerful man in Washington County. The elder Percy had long prided himself on his kind treatment of blacks. He knew he could not survive without their labor, and he tried his best

Hoover (left) traveled to the flood-damaged areas to help the victims of the flood, which included many children.

to keep them happy and safe. For decades, black people had fared better in Washington County than anywhere else in Mississippi. But when LeRoy Percy learned of his son's plan to evacuate the refugees, he was horrified. If they were evacuated, they might never return. Who would be left to till the fields? Who would harvest the cotton? Pressured by other prominent planters, LeRoy Percy mobilized the cotton growers and overturned his son's plans. When the boats arrived to take the refugees from the levee, Will Percy sent them away empty.

Once it was clear that the black refugees would not be evacuated, the levee became like a prison. Armed guards made sure that no one came or left without permission. Furthermore, Will and LeRoy Percy put the refugees to work without pay. Foremen with guns forced the refugees to load and unload supplies, dig latrines, and clean buildings that had been flooded. "The guard would come along and say, 'There's a boat coming up. Go unload,'" one woman said later. "If they didn't hurry up, they'd kick them. They didn't mind taking their pistols out and knocking them over the head."

Throughout the flooded areas, white refugees were treated very differently. They were sheltered indoors, in stores, warehouses, and churches. They received the best food the Red Cross could offer, from canned peaches to

THE ROAD TO THE WHITE HOUSE

Herbert Hoover was born in Iowa in 1874. Orphaned as a boy, he spent a lonely childhood moving from one relative to another. Later, he studied engineering at Stanford University in California. He made his fortune mining oil in Australia, China, Siberia, and Alaska. His work with victims of the Mississippi River flood earned him high praise in the U.S. press and helped launch his campaign for the presidency. Hoover was elected president of the United States in 1928, just before the country fell into a disastrous economic depression. Many blamed Hoover for the financial crisis, and he lost his bid for reelection in 1932.

★ ★ ★ ★

LeRoy Percy feared that if the refugees were evacuated, he would lose his workforce.

steaks. Such foods were not given to black refugees on the grounds that treats would "spoil" them. Above all, the white refugees were free to come and go at will. Soon most joined friends and relatives on higher ground.

In May, a black-owned newspaper, the *Chicago Defender*, ran a series of stories about abuses of blacks at Greenville and other refugee camps. Other northern papers picked up the story. Herbert Hoover feared that a scandal might shatter his reputation for kindness and good management. He appointed a team of black investigators to report on conditions in the camps. The report contained a number of criticisms, but Hoover ordered them softened in the final draft. Hoover assured the public that black refugees were treated fairly, and that all was well with the relief programs on the Mississippi. He also promised to push for the advancement of blacks if he was elected president.

THE LEGACY OF THE FLOOD

Inch by inch, day by day, the floodwaters receded. By the end of the summer, most of the flooded land was clear. A thick layer of stinking mud covered streets and fields. Mud caked the floors and walls of houses. Attracted by the dampness, snakes, insects, and spiders infested homes and stores. Gutters were clogged with millions of dead crayfish, decaying in the summer heat. The task of cleaning up after the disaster was overwhelming. Yet the survivors of the flood refused to let the river defeat them. Resolutely they mopped out their homes and reopened their businesses. They cleaned their streets and prepared to plant new crops the following summer.

The Red Cross claimed that 250 people died in the flood, but other estimates put the death toll at more than 1,000. The economic cost of the disaster has been tallied at $250

million to $500 million. In today's dollars, that would be $2.5 billion to $5 billion. Businessmen, politicians, and ordinary citizens wanted to be sure such a calamity never happened again. In May 1928, President Calvin Coolidge signed a bill called the Flood Control Act. The bill authorized the Army Corps of Engineers to expand and enlarge the entire flood control system. Levees would be heightened and strengthened from Cairo, Illinois, to the Gulf of Mexico, and along most of the Mississippi's tributaries. In addition, engineers would finally heed the advice Eads and Humphreys gave fifty years before. By 1936, spillways and reservoirs were in place to divert excess water when pressure on the levees began to build. The levees-only approach was abandoned forever.

★ ★ ★ ★

In the summer of 1928, the Republican Party chose Herbert Hoover to run for president of the United States. Hoover's relief work on behalf of the flood survivors had kept him in the national spotlight for months. No major scandal had erupted about mistreatment of black refugees at the Greenville levee. Hoover won the presidential election by a landslide.

To keep black laborers from leaving the Mississippi Delta, LeRoy Percy and his son had resorted to force. In the end, their efforts were to no avail. After the flood, thousands of blacks abandoned the South. Chicago, Detroit, and other northern cities beckoned with the promise of jobs and the chance to begin a new life. By 1930, 40 percent of the black labor force had left the delta.

As the floodwaters drained away, the people of St. Bernard and Plaquemines parishes struggled to collect their promised compensation. The business community of New Orleans set one obstacle after another in their way. Lawyers found loopholes that let the bankers break their agreement. Judges made a series of rulings against the families who had been evacuated. After a year of meetings and paperwork, the **claimants**—people who claimed damages—received an average of $284 apiece. Some were granted nothing at all.

The people of the flooded parishes were angry and disillusioned. They wanted someone in power to hear their voices. A fiery young politician named Huey Long seemed to listen to them and take their problems seriously. Long had grown up poor. He understood how it felt to scratch out

In the summer of 1928, the Republican Party chose Herbert Hoover to run for president of the United States. That fall, he won the election.

a living from the land. After a wildly successful campaign in Plaquemines, St. Bernard, and other poor parishes throughout the state, Huey Long was elected governor of Louisiana in 1928. The New Orleans business community never fully regained its power.

Huey Long appealed to the people affected by the floods because he grew up poor and knew what it was like to struggle. He was elected governor of Louisiana in 1928.

Beyond the political damage and even the physical cost, the very face of the region forever changed. The floodwaters of 1927 were as unforgiving in their effects on people as they were on the land. Since then, human efforts have largely succeeded in keeping the Mississippi under control. The mighty giant sleeps, though fitfully at times. Its human neighbors go about their business in peace. But they must remain watchful, ever alert to warning signs. Someday, the giant may awaken again.

DELTA BLUES

The blacks who headed north after the flood carried few possessions. But they took with them a form of music that had deep roots in the Mississippi Delta—the Delta blues. Delta blues performers sang of hardship, loss, and survival. Many songs were composed about the flood and the grueling work on the levees. Delta blues became immensely popular in Chicago and other northern cities.

A barge moves along the Mississippi River, which continues to be a major North American water route.

41

Glossary

barrow pit—deep, wide trench flanking a levee

batture—a broad floodplain between a riverbank and a levee

channel—the bed where a stream or river runs

claimants—people who claim they have been damaged in a disaster or accident

compensated—repaid for a loss or injury

crests—swiftly moving waves where a river is at its highest

crevasse—a break in a levee that allows river water to flood the land

delta—fertile land near the mouth of a river, built up by deposits of silt

diving bell—an early device for breathing underwater

levee—an earthen wall built along a river to prevent flooding

parishes—counties in the state of Louisiana

refugees—people left homeless by a flood or other natural disaster

sharecroppers—landless farmers who rented land from, and worked for, wealthy planters

silt—earth, sand, pebbles, and other debris washed downstream by a river

snags—clumps of tangled tree branches and logs washed downstream by a river

spillways—trenches to carry excess water away from a river

tributaries—branches that feed water to a larger river

Timeline: The Great

1541	1726	1879	1926	1927

1541 — Hernando de Soto and his expedition are the first Europeans to see the Mississippi River in its channel.

1726 — The people of New Orleans build the first levees to protect them from Mississippi floods.

1879 — The U.S. Congress creates the Mississippi River Commission to control flooding on the river; the commission chooses to build more levees and to close off natural outlets.

1926 — Unusually heavy rains fall in the Midwest; General Edgar Jadwin, chief of the Army Corps of Engineers, states that the Mississippi levees are strong enough to prevent future flooding.

1927

JANUARY–APRIL Work crews labor constantly to heighten and strengthen the levees as more rains fall; crevasses cause flooding in Illinois, Missouri, Arkansas, and Tennessee.

APRIL 21 A disastrous crevasse occurs near Mound Landing, Mississippi; more than 180,000 people are left homeless by flooding in Washington County.

Mississippi Flood of 1927

1928

1928–1930

APRIL 29
The Poydras Levee is dynamited, flooding St. Bernard and Plaquemines parishes in an attempt to spare New Orleans.

SUMMER
Some 13,000 black flood survivors are kept from leaving the levee near Greenville, Mississippi, and are forced to work without pay.

FALL
Floodwaters recede; flood survivors begin to clean up and go on with their lives.

MAY
The Flood Control Act places the Army Corps of Engineers in charge of a new flood-control project on the Mississippi.

NOVEMBER
Herbert Hoover is elected president of the United States; Huey Long is elected governor of Louisiana.

Thousands of black laborers leave the Mississippi Delta and head north to Chicago and other industrial cities.

To Find Out More

BOOKS

Blashfield, Jean F. *Red Cross and Red Crescent*. New York: World Almanac Library, 2003.

Blue, Rose J. *Exploring the Mississippi River Valley*. Milwaukee, Wis.: Raintree, 2004.

Duey, Kathleen. *Flood: Mississippi 1927*. New York: Aladdin, 1998.

Lourie, Peter. *Mississippi River: A Journey down the Father of Waters*. Old Millbrook, Conn.: Boyds Mill, 2002.

McNeese, Tim. *Rivers in American Life and Times: Mississippi River*. New York: Chelsea House, 2004.

ONLINE SITES

American Red Cross Museum: History Timeline
http://www.redcross.org/museum/timemach.html

National Geographic News: Great Flood
http://news.nationalgeographic.com/news/2001/05/0501_river4.html

PBS American Experience—Fatal Flood:
A Story of Greed, Power, and Race
http://www.pbs.org/wgbh/amex/flood

U.S. Army Corps of Engineers
http://www.usace.army.mil/

Index

About the Author

Deborah Kent grew up in Little Falls, New Jersey. She graduated from Oberlin College and received a master's degree from Smith College School for Social Work. For four years, she was a social worker at University Settlement House on New York's Lower East Side. In 1975, Ms. Kent moved to San Miguel de Allende in Mexico, where she wrote her first young-adult novel, *Belonging*. In San Miguel, Ms. Kent helped to found the Centro de Crecimiento, a school for children with disabilities.

Ms. Kent is the author of more than a dozen young-adult novels and numerous nonfiction titles for children. She lives in Chicago with her husband, children's author R. Conrad Stein, and their daughter, Janna.